Brandon Som, *Babel's Moon*
SELECTED BY AIMEE NEZHUKUMATATHIL

Stacey Waite, *the lake has no saint*
SELECTED BY DANA LEVIN

John Cross, *staring at the animal*
SELECTED BY GILLIAN CONOLEY

Cecilia Woloch, *Narcissus*
SELECTED BY MARIE HOWE

Joy Katz, *The Garden Room*
SELECTED BY LISA RUSS SPAAR

Mark Yakich, *The Making of Collateral Beauty*
SELECTED BY MARY RUEFLE

David Hernandez, *A House Waiting for Music*
SELECTED BY RAY GONZALEZ

Barbara Tran, *In The Mynah Bird's Own Words*
SELECTED BY ROBERT WRIGLEY

"*Night Logic* is an exquisite suite of poems rendering a family challenged by loss. In the aftermath, a young son becomes a de facto father to his younger brother. And a mother becomes a tragic and heroic figure. Matthew Gellman illuminates this dark domestic space while the speaker of these poems struggles with bullying, violence and his own sexuality. The poems in *Night Logic* are both mythic and grounded, formidable in their affection and insight."

DENISE DUHAMEL
Judge for the Snowbound Chapbook Award

The poems in *Night Logic* deal with queer coming-of-age and desire, as well as the persistent impact that childhood trauma can have on queer relationship-building. Focusing on the speaker's longing to be seen, as well as his frequent desire to hide, *Night Logic* charts the speaker's journey out of the closet and into an adult world that is both daunting and liberating at once. These confessional poems use the natural imagery of the speaker's childhood to evoke longing and loss, as the landscape around him functions as both mirror and conduit. Again and again, the poems analyze the role that the closet has played in his struggles with self-articulation, as well as his parents' divorce and the ways in which that rupture disorients him in his search for connection (romantic or otherwise). *Night Logic* explores the psychology of suppression in lucid, cinematic detail, presenting an elegant portrait of the pain that often comes with individuation.

NIGHT LOGIC

NIGHT LOGIC

POEMS

MATTHEW GELLMAN

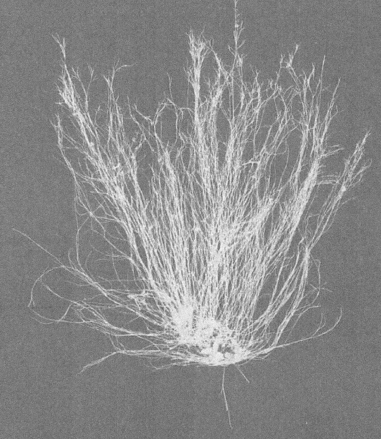

TUPELO PRESS

Tupelo Press
P.O. Box 1767
North Adams, Massachusetts 01247
(413) 664-9611 / Fax: (413) 664-9711
editor@tupelopress.org / www.tupelopress.org

Tupelo Press is an award-winning independent literary press that publishes fine
fiction, non-fiction, and poetry in books that are a joy to hold as well as read. Tupelo
Press is a registered 501(c)(3) nonprofit organization, and we rely on public support
to carry out our mission of publishing extraordinary work that may be outside the
realm of the large commercial publishers. Financial donations are welcome and are
tax deductible.

CONTENTS

NIGHT LOGIC

REPLICA

I wear a gray sweater not unlike the one
my father used to wear, his beard beginning
to hang from his face in his student years,
dew pooling on the sleeves. I see him
walking the autumned campus with a cone
of chrysanthemums flaring in his hand,
swaddled in newspaper wrapping, each petal
slanted a little, as memory is. It's easier
to go back this far, past the marriages,
past mornings of dressing for work
in the dark, his voice slick with caffeine,
mud on the front lawn clinging
to each jaded step. I'd rather remember
this sapling: my father, nineteen,
knocking on a woman's green door,
and the way the self emerges in the noon-lit
stillness just before it hears the word *yes*.
In this one life with its boundaries
set by snow, its laws cemented by air,
all we get is a moment to think
that we are permitted more than a moment.
I bought it, this cheap sweater the color
of sleep, a little worn at the shoulders.
It is not beautiful like the past
but like the past I wear it.

LITTLE BROTHER

In the photo of the blue raft I don't remember
you are reaching one arm out, staring

straight at our mother, whose hands
do not yet shake when holding a camera.

This is the past where nobody flinches,
the moment you climb away from our brother

becoming the moment where always
you will climb away from the shadow of his hand.

You do not know that in nine more winters
to please the voices in the attic of my mind

I will throw into the frost-storm
every suit our father owns, will toss

the locked-in pageant of the music box,
relic from before the disaster,

its dancer a flock of electric lines cut,
and you will gather what I've offered to snow.

You don't yet know that while our mother
will sleep, blanketed all season by shock,

past the wrecked spires of topiaries
I will drive you home from school,

waiting in the carpool line, hot breath
of a song I don't know on the back of my neck

and seeing your head in its red hat lowered
as the families around you assemble.

But in this photo it is not yet winter,
in this photo what exists is not the future

but only the gesture toward it
and not the fact of our father's leaving,

only his white shirt rippling over your chest
the second the yellow pail rolls away

as you turn to the balled fist of a wave
and squint, trying to see him.

MOTHER, SLEEVELESS

She walks home from the all girls' Catholic school
under the thumb of March, arms crossed, petals
grazing her shoulders, wind pushed into her mouth.
She knows this street: its laundry lines heavy
with pigeons. Parked cars. The gutter's rough music.
It's the fastest way, but all month the winter
has taken too long to lie down. She wants to be
alone, but a carful of boys swings around the corner
of Erdrich, banging the windshield and shouting,
tobacco wet between their teeth. She starts to run
from their voices, the gray street and the car horn's
sallow bleating, the empty shirts on her neighbors'
lines making emptier shadows across their lawns.
She does what she's already learned to do:
she holds down her skirt and runs deeper into
the life I will enter, its same dark colors
and the maples cold, beginning.

BROTHER, AGE SIX

Before the tenuous muslin of her marriage
had flickered away, before the piano,

one morning, you and I were becoming
in our mother's favorite shoes. Left alone

in summer, the house emptied, our nightshirts
draped to our knees, we went to her closet:

open boxes, the pumps glossy, upright
prizes. You imitated her, sauntering

across the cream-colored carpet
until you fell. Then when I fell over you

we laughed until you pushed me off.
You looked and said, *Do you sometimes*

wanna go someplace else. I said, *Where.*
Then you stood up in your heels and practiced.

HOMECOMING

I wanted to shine. To make
my body burn. To unlock

every glass case where I used
to store all my silences

and watch them pirouette
onto the cedar floor.

A brightness in the kitchen,
a willow holding sunset

in the hoop of its dress—
while my mother set the table,

I heard my father's car
surrender in the driveway.

It took so long for me
to understand why,

each time, she turned away—
shame for having bought

the gown for me, for wishing
I'd been a daughter.

I wore pink tulle. I spun
until I could no longer see

my father, in the doorway,
his head in his hand.

THE WHEAT FIELD

i.
I came to the wheat field
to look for my sister
but my sister was not there
there was only sunlight
fanning the silence
and getting all over
the things that it owned
and the taste of the sunlight
the taste a white linen
dress pulled over my head
and each time I turn
to look closer at myself
I turn from myself.

ii.
As a girl my mother
didn't like to dance.
At night, she walked
around those blocks
of row-homes standing
like graves in soil,
avoiding the gymnasium.
She reached a parking lot

overgrown with grass
where she could lie down,
unflooded by headlights.
Could think. Could look
at the imperfect animal
stillness of every star.

iii.
At the school dance I stood
almost ghost at the edge
of the purple lights.
Then, being driven home,
words were heavy-footed
and the field almost broken
by blizzard. But I still thought
I could point out the few soft crops
still cowering in their stalks,
my face always looking
for something beating inside
what was hardly there.

iv.
I come to the wheat field
to look for my sister
but my sister is not here,
my sister is somewhere
asleep in the sun inside her;

my sister lives only inside.
She will never see this night
will not find me watching
these airplanes disappear.
I don't know where they're going
but I watch them go.

The day a boy was discovered
roped to a fence, his body an emblem
of caution, the cyclist who found him there
mistook him for a scarecrow,

so pistol-whipped and transfigured by blood
his Wyoming face, his blonde fingers
still moving, trying to praise
the modicum of breeze.

To be queer is to be questioned
on the way your breathing
displaces light. The way you lilt
or stutter. The way a cigarette learns

to bleed from your hand. I was that boy's age
when a man tried to follow me home
in the clapboard college town
where I made submersible

in the weave of roots next to
a crippled fence. According to gestalt theory
the whole is greater than the sum
of its parts. One light tapped on

on the railroad track
becomes all the lights interrupting
the cold. By this night logic
a boy jumps over a fence

or a boy gets bound to the fence
and there is only an aperture of dead grass
to determine the difference.
The man searches but he cannot find me

and stumbles down the mess
of the alley. I keep my head low
and wait for the morning to steady.
So quiet I hear the whole planet.

A boy is a galaxy shoved underwater.
A moon with a fork in its sternum.
A boy is a star in the stratosphere
blinking like something that could be extinguished.

Twin hornets, you and I raced the living room, playing our game of chase
until you tumbled jumping the back of the armchair, your left leg
snapping on the carpet, the ligament swarming with purple, the shin
splitting off from the thigh. The cast was chronic for a season,
jagged rainbows scribbled onto it, affirmations, stick-figure flowers
and the names of the kids in our class at school. The same boys
who would later spit on my cheek and throw me onto the blacktop,
looming, the shadows of hemlocks erasing their steps as they turned
to go. I learned to seek refuge in the tough Pennsylvania field,
yellow weed and spurge, in the bleak apprehensions of crows
as they skimmed the pond, not accusing but not kind. You learned
to recover, dragging your shell of a shin through the den, wringing
your hands, encircled by a tentative light that will always return me
to injury. *Hey*, you call to me from a leaf-pile, healed, October
simmering behind you, *You bury me first and then you let me bury you.*

SMOKE

Shame obeys its own ritualism
in this too-bright light of Chinatown
where father sits with his chest square,
claiming the darkest meat

of the bird. Mother says if I curl
my knuckles inward I must not be a fag,
that if I push my hands out straight
when checking my nails

I'm the wrong kind of boy.
I thought I could trick each digit,
achieve the posture
and freeze the questioning there

like the russet skin
of the static ducks left
dangling in the windows,
this test just three days after

the boys pelted me with orange peels
on the playground I wandered, ill-
fitting, solitude becoming
a slate nail in my throat.

A little grubby
with duck sauce,
aiming for reversal
of the unhoped-for reveal,

not perfectly studied in how
to perform a masculine front,
my fingers descend
while behind their flutter

of side-eye, there is smoke, a flame
being tempered, mother and father's
adult minds discussing
what they might do about me.

Should I have taken more notes
about the pig's legs, pickled on the tray?
About the blonde fingers of the girl
I'd been partnered with, her scalpel
slitting the heart? I walked home
after class and stared at the stipples
in the field, the radish flanks of the horse
lit by a rain I could only describe
as sudden. I'd been ashamed to not
make the cut through that skin,
toughened and grayed by the freezer,
the pig's eyes pressed in a squint
as if even in death she could feel
what was coming. So I let the girl
do it. She held down the throat
with its tiny, barely perceptible hairs,
steadied the slightly puckering body
and told me *It's fine, I've done it before.*
But in a boy's mind, what is absent
enlarges to make up a landscape:
spring, desiccated. Another boy, shirt
on the carpet. Light overtaking
the classroom that morning, spilling
through the acacia in the window,

pouring over the anatomy textbook
and settling in the pig's bright aperture,
all of her insides shining, like anything
severed. We spend life trying to grow
either harder or softer, and mostly
just wanting reprieve; even the horse
seems to know this, watching me
walk fast again down the road,
having looked for long enough
at this animal muffled in the pen
to imagine its body asleep, hauled
onto the slab, still steaming in rain.

My mother was younger than I am now
when she rode the bus to the Halloween party,
the lights veering red yellow green

on the dance floor where my father,
a stranger then, pulls the styrofoam clown nose
off her face and puts it on his own,

then walks off without her even trying
to chase his sweaty back or his brashness.
Since I first heard this story

I've often wanted to keep my mother
inside it. Wearing those baggy pants,
a brown drink rocking inside her plastic cup.

I like to think I was perched on the rafters
or a seedling in the barroom plant,
pin-sized pupil watching their meeting

from the fern's nucleus of unfurling.
I see it so clearly I must have been there—
my father turning to look at my mother,

fanning the slow conflagrations
of their lives that will deliver my own,
goading us into the game

of need, projection and scar

that will crack and recover
my twenty-nine years

repeatedly, like a dropped glass marble.
Their voices soft with beer,
two animals staring each other down

under strobe lights, the garble of music
between them, something withheld:
here I learn the template.

That night cannot unexist.
I am proof of it. I am still inside it.
So invisible I must be everywhere.

SNIPE

His low, madrone-colored drumming
skitters over the knotted tuft of marsh
like a siren skimming the unkempt
songs on the insides of our throats
thirsting for sun. I love watching him
dip his enormously long beak
in the water, all of his camouflage
ruffled, wading in before stuttering
into another swoop toward the mountain.
When it was clear that my father
would not come back, my mother began
making lists: where to throw out
his clothes, where to get the pills,
the places his hands had been.
She substituted food for Virginia Slims
and at night tugged the phone off its hook.
She pulled the fern from its socket
and threw its frenzy of hair on the floor.
Sometimes, on the patio, singing
the songs that made her feel like a girl
again, I would fumble the chorus
and the same notes began riding
the starless heat of our mouths,
and though this didn't call him back,

though we knew it wouldn't, though
we could barely look at each other
this is how I've used my voice since then:
not to be beautiful, not to contend with
whatever question each season is singing,
not even to try to convince anyone
I am sane and going to be all right,
but more like the snipe veering over
this soggy meadow, calling out to no one,
just using his voice to know that he is here.

I am thinking of the sister I wish I had,
red hair spilling over the sedan's back seat
as a boy speeds her through the blue vein
of suburb and out toward the cedar forest.
Her finger hooked in the hole burned into the seat
by someone's boyfriend's ash, her head
tilted back, lulled by the driver's junky radio:
Nothing's gonna hurt you, baby, as long as you're with me.
Even now, after years of trying to see her
striding into dusk, all beforelight, all promise,
her dress a galloping of small yellow wings,
my mind still delivers me only this:

that group of boys killing their engine
and doing to her under the cedars' nimbus
things I will not say in this poem.
Not unlike the boy who held me underwater
in his swimming pool, July, his parents
not home, his whole body locked around me
as he pulled off my trunks, how even now
I can feel a small finger twisting my throat
when I try to tell it, if I were to tell it
completely, if I had a sister to tell.

When I find her along that highway
all her hair will be cut off. She will not speak
all summer and no kite will flutter
in her hands. But in winter, her hair
regrown, she will ask me to drive her
to that forest again, and clutching my arm
in hers, she will look out at the field
that broke her, not trying to say anything,
just rocking back and forth for a little while,
silent as the tundra glittering before us.

BROTHER, IN AUGUST, WITH HESITATION

Wanting to be untethered from the burden
of pollen, the garden drowsy with asters,

we went upstairs, taking turns wetting
and smoothing our hair in the bathroom mirror.

We lined up, the other boys comparing,
deciding which of us had the best nose or skin,

inspecting our teeth with a magnifying glass
we'd trawled from some bin in the basement,

and it was our contest, getting a point
for the deepest voice, a point for being

the tallest, a point for which one of us
we thought we could trust to never tell.

I could not have told you about those nights
years later, in the starling weather,

when myself and one of those boys
would slink the fractured emerald veil

of the pond, wiping the sweat
from my forehead, stilling my voice,

the light in your room extinguished
as we kissed beside an urgency of geese,

wings flaring up, re-enfolding to black.
You and I never could tell each other

that in those stammering attic lights
we shared the same coveting:

the rough palm, the panting, the real thing,
the blessing of being chosen by a boy.

And you couldn't have told who he was,
at school, quiet in the varicose hallways,

his eyes at lunchtime fixed on the trees
because it was easier, looking at trees.

SPECIAL REPORT, AFTER RAIN

What's left is the sound of my father's shirt
            as it stiffens on the line. Is the long
                        professorial praying mantis

puttering the garden, glossed
            in moonlight, waiting for dinner
                        to appear and the TV rages:

men in kevlar, slithering the pocked-
            up desert for oil and uranium.
                        When he was home, my father

would watch these reports
            in our living room each night,
                        air strikes, drone strikes, a family

shot dark in a car, the incinerated
            minds of caves. What I have left
                        is the sound of his suitcase

clattering down the stairs.
            Is his face lit up as it studied
                        other faces being overriden

by flame. The thrashing, the factless

      thrust, the barrel cocked

            by someone else's son,

never the quiet gesturer pausing

      to look up at the bulletless moon.

            I stood barefoot in the wet grass

to watch this smaller hunter

      devour the aphid, killing to stay

            alive, killing only because it must.

TYLER

He'd get off work at the bar and come over late
and adjust his flat-brimmed hat. He'd say *I'm sorry*
I've been the worst. Then he'd say *I want to rip you*
open. He'd talk of his hatred for New Jersey, firewood
rotting on the porch, his mother's dumb husband.
When I told him, drunk, I think we're all here to do
something, he said he didn't really know. He was called
maricón at his last job and his friends live scattered
all over, and this year on Mother's Day, when he fought
with his mother, he threw the azaleas he'd bought
on the doormat. Once, he said that his brother
and his friends poured a bucket of ice on his head
in the garden, holding his legs down, his mother
in the kitchen, salting the dinner and not intervening,
and, once, Tyler watched from the grass as the boys
poked an injured bird with a stick on the pavement
for half an hour, the bird trying to haul itself back
into wind with one infuriated wing. So it makes sense
that Tyler keeps moving from one red-throated city
to another. It makes sense that Tyler's first boyfriend
only fucked him from behind. And I can see why Tyler
stumbles when he walks, even with wide open space,
and why he only fucks me from behind, at my apartment,
over the boxspring, and late. What we fill with our sadness

we end up tearing a little, sometimes all the way open,
no matter how we want to fix the broken architecture
of wings. For every bird baking on asphalt there's a boy
years later, far from home, filling another boy's bedroom
with the softer parts of himself that Tyler wanted me
to see. Feeling my hands pulled straight back behind me,
my face avoiding its reflection in the window, I think
yes, we are all meant for something, and Tyler left
something out of the story: the part where the creature
accepts it, where its body just stops attempting the air,
where it's wiser to lie down into the pain, to get
comfortable choosing the ground.

WATCHING THE HERON WITH MY MOTHER,

I REMEMBER APERTURES

All afternoon we wait for something
to happen to the river. Then the heron,

great blue, with miserly neck and legs,
arranges its shadow on a rock,

not dissimilar to a boy in a Greek myth
staring at his black undercarriage of earth,

the centrifuge of its two prongs ready
to skewer the least careful fish.

I'm remembering the better nights now,
watching alfalfa fields popping up

from my used Honda, the family
dissolved, my feminine traits

no longer a mockery, and how
nothing could make us drive back

to that house, the answers
each of its rooms couldn't give, grief

the frigid milk of swans
shaking cages in our minds.

We did not talk about time then,
needles of fireflies re-sewing the night,

silence always a native tongue
we abandon and return to together.

We do not talk about time. We stare
at the river quickened by trout, the heron

searching for some sort of talisman,
for something to make its own.

There are so many questions the rain in a city
will always turn into answers. *Will there be flooding*
becomes: *Of course. Why didn't he come back*

becomes: *He didn't.* But you remember mornings
mimicking the couples you'd seen in movies.
How his hair looked tied in a bun. How he'd use

words like proclivity. You met him at a party upstate
and walked home together, passing a muffled campfire,
shapes painted on the water tower, joints scattered

like the season's first flowers. He looked down,
as boys often do when telling the truth about themselves.
It was like that then. He wiped the grass from his jeans.

Now the city is teeming, and you still haven't gone
anywhere. His umbrella still coiled in the closet;
your bedroom blown cold by the unfinished fact

of winter. This is how it works: the window
gets stuck, it lets in the rain's darkening language
and you spend an afternoon trying too hard to close it.

SAINT TIMOTHY'S SCHOOL, 1975

It is natural for us to want to be cradled
says the nun who clutches the fake toy baby
after rapping your open palm with a ruler
for being late to Home Economics.
You scuttle toward the back of the classroom
and cannot help but notice, mother, the dense
relief of the gray trees riddled with white sun
emptying each of snow. Your mind knows
how to carry you far, alert but sullen
in your household, half-asleep on your feet
as you spread jam and cheese onto bread
for your father, or sulking on your walks home,
asymmetrical whirr of light leaking out of the bars
that same light I passed in my twenties,
upstate New York, summer fully turned on.
The night a green bottle hurtled past my ear
and smashed on the pavement in front of me
I'd just left a gay bar to smoke and watch dragonflies
sputter out in the cracks on the sidewalk.
I froze as the men drove off, murmuring
fag, accelerating into the blackness
as the beer-foam rivered out, collapsing
like the rhetoric of this performative era.
Our loneliness is a lineage heavy as a heatwave,

inevitable as a blizzard, and though
I rarely admit this, mother, that night
I'd have liked to be scooped by your hands,
hands that tied your hair tight for the journey
so you could endure the whoosh of cold
and the passing cars and the passing jeers
of the boys who rode inside them.
Shaking into myself this morning, I see
the grimness of swans on water,
hovering girls in a rectory, feathers
fastened to an ineffable wind.
I have never prayed at St. Timothy's Cathedral
or stared at his face in edifice,
but according to the scripture
he was a timid, compassionate man.

Would you spit like me. Would you wear
your hair in braids. Would you smoke
Marlboro Reds. Would you swear.
Would you wish you were blonde.
Would you stutter. Would you know
our mother. What instrument would you
play. What boys would look at you.
Would you look back. Would you teach me
how to roll my pants, how to paint
my nails. Would our father know you.
Would he drive you to prom. Would you
dress me as a girl. Could we wear
purple lipstick. Would you teach me
how to push out my hip, how to play
hopscotch. Would you sing. Would you
give advice: should I meet the boy
under the bleachers. Would you wait
by the chain-link fence the whole time,
crushing dandelions. Would you tell.
Would you take me home and not
ask questions. Would I lose track,
would you walk ahead, night-brush
cutting the same shapes into our knees.

ACKNOWLEDGEMENTS

The Adroit Journal: "Homecoming"; "Trying to Grow"; "Watching the
  Heron with my Mother, I Remember Apertures"; "Tyler"
Beloit Poetry Journal: "Smoke"
Frontier Poetry: "Night Logic"
Harpur Palate: "Mother, Sleeveless"
Indiana Review: "Brother with Rupture"
The Los Angeles Review: "The Wheat Field"
Narrative Magazine: "Replica"
The Nashville Review: "Little Brother"
New South: "Brother, in August, with Hesitation"
Nimrod International Journal: "Cloudburst"
Ninth Letter: "Snipe"
Passages North: "Beforelight"
Poetry Northwest: "Sister, Far Ahead"
Tinderbox Poetry Journal: "Brother, Age Six"
Tupelo Quarterly: "Special Report, After Rain"
Waxwing: "Saint Timothy's School, 1975"

MATTHEW GELLMAN is a 2022-2023 National Endowment for the Arts Fellow. His poems have appeared in *Poetry Northwest, Narrative, The Common, Ninth Letter, Indiana Review,* Lambda Literary's Poetry Spotlight, the *Missouri Review, Waxwing,* and elsewhere. Matthew's debut poetry collection, *BEFORELIGHT,* was selected by Tina Chang as the winner of the 22nd annual A. Poulin, Jr. Poetry Prize and is forthcoming from BOA Editions, Ltd. The recipient of awards and honors from Brooklyn Poets, the Academy of American Poets, the Adroit Journal's Djanikian Scholars Program and the New York State Summer Writers Institute, he holds an MFA from Columbia University and lives in Brooklyn.